SIX SIGMA

Step-by-Step Guide to Six Sigma

(Six Sigma Tools, DMAIC, Value Stream Mapping, Launching a Project and Implementing Six Sigma)

Jason Bennett & Jennifer Bowen

Table of Contents

Introduction

As a business concept, Six Sigma has been around for decades. However, for most of that time, many organizations viewed Six Sigma with a bit of suspicion. There was this myth that Six Sigma was simply a methodology that slowed down a business process and didn't really produce much fruit.

Thankfully, things have changed. Today, Six Sigma has been embraced and appreciated for its numerous benefits and as a way of helping organizations achieve their strategic goals.

On the other hand, there is still a lot that most people don't understand about Six Sigma.

There may be a lot of books and articles out there about this topic, but most of these resources can be quite complicated and difficult to read. They don't present Six Sigma in a way that is simple and easy enough to understand for most interested readers.

However, this book is different. In this book, *Six Sigma*, I will introduce you to Six Sigma and the philosophy and principles that form its foundation. You will also learn some of the main tools and processes that are used in a Six Sigma framework, namely DMAIC and Value Stream Mapping.

I also break down the key steps that you need to follow to identify and implement a Six Sigma project. Some of the mistakes that you need to avoid during Six Sigma implementation are also highlighted in this book.

The goal of this book is to help you understand the main principles and steps of setting up a Six Sigma project. Once you have gained this kind of knowledge, you will be able to confidently move forward to integrate Six Sigma into your organizational culture. You will be able to improve your business processes and cut down on any delays and wastage that may exist in your business.

So, are you ready to begin?

Happy reading!

Chapter One: Understanding Six Sigma

Most people believe that a company exists only to create profit. However, this is not exactly true. If you were to ask any CEO of a successful corporation why their organization exists, they would tell you that their main purpose is to create value for their constituents.

In other words, a business exists to serve the owners, shareholders, and customers. This value is created by utilizing the available resources and generating outputs that are greater in value than the inputs. This entire process chain cannot be profitable unless the business processes are effective and efficient.

So what does all this have to do with Six Sigma?

In this chapter, you are going to learn how Six Sigma can be used to ensure that the business process generates maximum value at a minimum cost. You will discover the philosophy and principles behind this methodology and some of the benefits incurred when Six Sigma is adopted in an organization.

Defining Six Sigma

Six Sigma can be defined as a system of statistical-based tools, techniques, and methodologies that are designed to eliminate defects and errors in products and services while minimizing process variability.

A defect is anything that does not meet the customer's expectations. In simple terms, Six Sigma is a system that ensures that your business produces products and services are of a *consistently* high quality.

If you take a good look at the business world today, you will realize that every organization worth its salt maintains an online presence. Since we live in the information age, news tends to spread like wildfire. Therefore, companies have been forced to raise the quality of their goods and services, lest a disgruntled customer grabs their phone and tweets or posts a comment about bad service.

Businesses must now guard their reputations and brands by making sure that they consistently provide products and services that meet the customer's needs. Of all the possible quality systems available, it is Six Sigma that has been accepted as the standard.

But how does this relate to performance?

Sigma is usually represented by the Greek letter, σ, and refers to a measure of variability. If you want to determine the performance of a business, all you have to do is measure the sigma level of the processes it uses. It is important to understand that every process has an average or mean value.

Any deviation from the mean is considered undesirable, but since no product or service is perfect, some allowance needs to be made. This is why the Six Sigma process is divided into six standard deviations from the process average.

We have 1 σ, 2 σ, 3 σ, and so on until the maximum of 6 σ. Most companies usually have processes that perform at 3 or 4 σ, but the goal of every company is to attain a level of 6 σ, which is based on defects per million opportunities.

The standard for Six Sigma is 3.4 defects per million opportunities. However, the good news is that even if you do not attain the 6 σ level, any improvements you make between 3 σ to 5 σ will lead to a substantial decrease in costs and an increase in customer satisfaction.

The Philosophy Behind Six Sigma

Six Sigma is a scientific methodology, and as such, you must use scientific techniques when developing your business processes and systems. It is these scientific techniques that the employees will use to improve the value of the products and services.

This will ultimately benefit both the customers as well as the shareholders.

As a philosophy, Six Sigma embraces the idea that every individual business process can be measured and then improved. Here is a simplified way of looking at how the Six Sigma philosophy is used in a business:

1. The company identifies one key aspect of its business, maybe a process that is considered to be underperforming.

2. A hypothesis is developed. This hypothesis must be consistent with what is being observed.

3. The company runs some experiments to confirm their observations about the process. As more observations come to light and fresh data is recorded, the hypothesis is adjusted.

4. Statistical methods are used to separate real data from noise.

5. Steps 2, 3, and 4 are repeated until the hypothesis matches the actual results.

If the company continues to follow this system over an extended period of time, it will be able to come up with a theory or model that enables it to easily understand every internal business process as well as its customers.

The end result is that instead of making decisions based on hypotheses or guesswork, management will begin to rely on hard data.

Though most organizations think that they operate on real data, the truth is that they do not. Some are simply being run based on traditions.

This is why you will hear a manager say, "That's how we have always done things around here, and it works."

Yet the reality is that a company that focuses on using the Six Sigma approach systematically and consistently will improve its performance over time and leave the rest drowning in its wake.

Principles of Six Sigma

To guarantee success when using Six Sigma, you have to learn these five key principles:

1. Customer focus

Before you improve the quality of a product or service, you must first define the word "quality." The best person to define what quality means is not you but your customer. Therefore, focus on the feedback from your customers and adjust your processes accordingly.

2. Identification of causes of variations

When you are dealing with a business process, you need to understand that variation is your enemy. Your products must be consistent in terms of quality. If customers cannot trust that what they buy today will be of the same quality tomorrow, they will flee to your business rivals.

The first step in identifying the root cause of a problem is to understand how the process works. Not how it is expected to work but how it actually works. To achieve this, you need to:

- Identify the kind of data you need to collect

- Clearly define why that data must be collected

- Clarify the information that the data will reveal

- Communicate the terms clearly

- Make sure that the measurements taken are precise and repeatable

- Develop a standardized system of data collection

Data collection is generally done by interviewing various stakeholders, observing the process, and asking the right questions. Examples of questions that you should ask include:

- What can we do to make your job easier?

- Why is this process done this way?

- Are there any tasks that you perform that seem unnecessary?

Once you have collected the data, use the information to find the underlying cause of variation.

3. Elimination of variation

The next step after identifying the root cause of variation is to eliminate the variation. To achieve this, you have to make adjustments to your business process.

These adjustments include eliminating any steps that don't add value to your customer. The end result will be the elimination of defects and minimization of wastage.

4. Teamwork

To ensure that Six Sigma is implemented properly, you need to have a diverse team that is committed to incorporating the Six Sigma methodologies. When a team has members with diverse skills, they will be able to detect variations in the different areas of the business process.

The team must be highly skilled and trained in the use of Six Sigma tools and techniques. There are five levels of Six Sigma certification. These are Master Black Belt, Black Belt, Green Belt, Yellow Belt, and White Belt. The highest certification is the master black belt.

5. Flexibility and thoroughness

To successfully implement Six Sigma in an organization, the system must be willing to accept change. Management and employees must be flexible in their thinking so that they see the benefits of the changes being implemented.

This means that the employees must be clearly informed about how the changes will affect their work. If they are consulted early, Six Sigma will be readily accepted.

The implementation itself must not be so complicated that people would rather stick working with a flawed process than move to the new one. You also need to make sure that you thoroughly understand every area of the process.

Benefits of Six Sigma

There are some companies that assume that they do not need Six Sigma because their business is doing well. However, they fail to realize the immense potential of the Six Sigma approach. Those companies that have applied these methodologies and techniques have experienced substantial positive changes and immense benefits.

Here are some of the major benefits of Six Sigma:

1. Improvement in quality – Earlier in this chapter, we defined a defect as anything that fails to meet the expectations of a customer. Though these expectations vary from one product/service to the next, it isn't that difficult for a company to know when one of its products or services has a defect. Six Sigma enables companies to reduce these defects as much as possible so that overall quality is improved. When this happens, more customers will enjoy the product or service.

2. Expanded innovation – If an organization wants to grow steadily and avoid stagnation, it must innovate. When Six Sigma came onto the scene, most companies believed that it would stifle innovation. However, the reverse has proven to be the case. Studies show that Six Sigma has promoted collaboration and new ideas in the companies that have embraced this methodology. Research shows that 46% of companies that implement Six Sigma see an improvement in innovation. One reason behind this is that the employees began focusing more on solutions instead of limitations.

3. Cost reduction – Six Sigma can save a company a lot of money by minimizing wastage and defects. The money saved can then be channeled elsewhere. For example, the US Army used the methodology in 2007 and managed to save a whopping $2 billion in that year alone. The army used Six Sigma to streamline some of its internal processes such as task management, fuel recycling, and dining hall scheduling.

4. Focus on a common goal – In most organizations, getting every member of staff to focus on the same goal can be a tall order. The different departments tend to have their own individual objectives, and the only thing they share is the need to deliver products, services, or information to the customers. Six Sigma, however, brings the entire organization together to focus on the single goal of achieving a near-perfect performance level. The performance standard set by Six Sigma is 99.9997 percent. This is extremely high, especially if you compare it with the 99 percent performance standard that many organizations normally aim for. For example, if a company manufactures 1000 trucks, a 99 percent performance standard would mean that 10 trucks would be defective. However, using the Six Sigma performance standard of 99.9997 percent, only 1 truck would have a defect!

5. Continuous learning – An organization that implements Six Sigma methodologies will be in a state of continuous learning. The employees will have access to the tools necessary for generating fresh ideas that turbocharge development and innovation. When employees are relocated from one sector of the organization to another, they bring with them a fresh perspective that will ultimately have a positive impact.

6. A boost in long-term revenue – When a company improves the quality of its products and services, it will experience an increase in its long-term revenue.

7. Enhances employee safety –Six Sigma always leads to a significant improvement in consistency and protocol within an organization. This is good for employee safety because employee working conditions get better. In fact, studies show that 56 percent of organizations that implement Six Sigma report an increase in employee safety. For example, a hospital that adopts the Six Sigma approach will be able to streamline laboratory processes. This will reduce the amount of lab staff overtime, thus saving the hospital a lot of money while also allowing staff to go home on time and rest. Employees who are well rested are less likely to make mistakes on the job.

As you have learned, Six Sigma is an effective and efficient approach that focuses on improving quality, reducing costs, and increasing revenues. In the next chapter, you will learn the main tools and processes used in Six Sigma.

Chapter Two: Six Sigma Tools and Processes

There are quite a number of tools and processes that are used within the Six Sigma methodology. In this chapter, you will learn what these tools are and how they work. You will also learn about some of the main frameworks that define Six Sigma.

DMAIC Tools

DMAIC is the main framework that Six Sigma relies upon during implementation. DMAIC is a performance improvement model that consists of five main phases. These are:

- Define phase – Defining the project

- Measure phase – Measuring the current performance/output of the project

- Analyze phase – Finding the causes of defects

- Improve phase - Creating solutions to minimize the number of defects

- Control phase – Monitoring performance and the new improvements

Each of the above phases incorporates specific tools and processes. These tools are very useful when identifying, analyzing, and improving problems.

It is important to understand that DMAIC tools should not be used haphazardly. You must know which tools to apply during the specific phases of the process.

We will go into greater detail about the DMAIC model and the steps involved in chapter 4. For now, let's focus on its tools and processes.

Tools for the Define phase

1. Project charter

A project charter is a document that is used to describe an entire project. It defines the objectives of the project, the management structure to be used, the main stakeholders, and their roles and responsibilities.

Keep in mind that when we talk about a project in Six Sigma, we are referring to the project that will improve the business process and eliminate defects.

There are several elements in a project charter. These include:

- Business case – This is the link between the project and the goals of the organization. The project must always fall in line with the organization's long-term goals.

- Problem statement – What is wrong with the current process? What will happen if the problem is not fixed? At this point, you do not need to provide a solution or apportion blame to particular parties.

- Goal statement – This is a statement that describes the goal of the project.

- Project scope – This is a description of the extent (length and breadth) of the project.

- Project milestones – These are the timelines for completing the various stages of the project.

2. SIPOC diagram – This is an illustration of the various activities that will be part of the improvement process. SIPOC stands for Supplier, Input, Process, Output, and Customer.

3. Process maps

This is a tool that visually illustrates how the various steps of the process are linked to each other. It generally includes:

- Deployment flowchart – This is a description of the roles and responsibilities of every stakeholder involved in the project.

- Process flowchart – This is a logical arrangement of project activities.

4. Critical-to-quality drill down tree – This tool is used to convert customer requirements into quantifiable characteristics.

5. Voice of the customer – This involves gathering feedback from customers regarding a particular product or service.

Tools for the Measure phase

1. Sampling – This is where you collect data by selecting a small number of elements from a bigger target group. There are different forms of sampling, such as cluster sampling, snowball sampling, simple random sampling, stratified random sampling, etc.

2. Process sigma calculation – This is a tool that is used when comparing the output of a process to a particular performance standard. A process that has a higher process sigma is considered to be more capable than one with a lower process sigma.

Tools for the Analysis phase

1. Why analysis – This tool consists of a series of "Why" questions that are asked to find out the reasons for defects and bottlenecks in a process.

2. Hypothesis testing – This tool is used for identifying the presence of statistical variations between two sets of data. You establish a null and alternate hypothesis, calculate the test statistics, and then interpret the results.

Tools for the Improve phase

1. Pilot solution implementation – As the name suggests, this is a tool that comes in handy when you need to test how effective a solution is before implementing it. It is especially useful when you are dealing with a project with a large scope of variability.

2. Failure mode effect analysis – As an analysis tool, FMEA is used whenever you need to find any potential points of failure within a process. If a failure mode is discovered, it is assigned a risk priority number, with 10 being the highest and 1 being the lowest risk. This risk priority number is then used to develop the appropriate contingency plans.

3. Brainstorming – Though it may sound a bit simplistic, brainstorming is actually a pretty effective tool when trying to improve a process. You can gather a bunch of specialists from different areas within an organization and brainstorm a list of reasons why a particular problem exists. These root causes are then ranked and selected according to their order of importance.

Tools for the Control phase

1. Control charts – This tool can be used to analyze or control a particular process. A control chart helps you identify any variations that may arise within a process. We all know that every process has some level of instability within it. This variation usually follows a predictable pattern. However, there are times when the variation becomes excessive, and therefore, a control chart is necessary to spot such occurrences. The organization can then take remedial action to prevent the process from becoming more chaotic.

Value Stream Mapping

Apart from the DMAIC tools discussed above, there are other alternatives that can be used during Six Sigma implementation. One of these is Value Stream Mapping. This is a graphical tool that shows how materials and information are flowing through an organization. A value stream map shows the current state of the value stream and how it would look like after the defects have been eliminated. It is quite useful when identifying and reducing waste in a process in order to achieve a smooth and effective flow.

For example, in a manufacturing company, a value stream map would be used to show all the value added to a product, from the raw materials all the way to the finished product that is eventually bought by a consumer.

Uses of a Value Stream Map

Value stream mapping serves the following functions:

- It illustrates how different organizational functions interact and how resources flow.

- It graphically depicts the defects, inefficiencies, bottlenecks, and problem areas in a process flow.

- It reveals the lag times and cycle times that occur between various tasks.

- It makes it easier to create and implement solutions that bring about a shift in organizational culture. For example, a value stream map will highlight all the stakeholders responsible for every stage of a business process and how change can be implemented.

- It facilitates continuous improvement by focusing on efficient transformational teams.

Creating a Value Stream Map

There are four key steps in making a value stream map:

1. Determining the current state of the process

2. Analyzing and reflecting on the current value stream map

3. Improving the process

4. Sustaining the improvements

Step one: Determine the current state

The first thing to do is to decide which product or process needs improvement. Once you have done this, you need to choose a cross-functional team to map how the process flows from start to finish. Every primary and secondary flow should be considered as well as any communication points.

In most cases, the project sponsor is the one who decides when a process starts and ends. However, during value stream analysis, the process is usually mapped from the moment a customer makes an order to the time they receive their order.

Then the entire process, including sub-steps, is mapped, and you end up with a process flow diagram. It is important to note the areas that involve inputs and outputs.

Once all the steps have been visually represented, you then determine which metrics will be measured for each step of the process. This is important because there are cases where some steps are too complex or costly to measure than others. Some of the metrics that you can use include:

- Average time

- Median time

- Changeover time

- Amount of resources

- Number of staff/manpower

- Capabilities of machinery

- Throughput

Collecting and measuring this kind of data will be time-consuming, so make sure you are precise the first time around. It would also be a good idea to test your preferred measuring tools before you begin.

Step two: Analyze and reflect

The second step is to sit down with all the stakeholders and examine the current state of the value stream map. The aim here is to get everyone to agree on the prevailing performance of the process. Once there is a consensus that the process must be improved, the defects and deficiencies need to be identified and their costs quantified.

The root causes of each defect must also be identified so that cost-effective solutions can be formed. Keep in mind that root causes are very different from mere symptoms, so avoid focusing on the symptoms of the defects.

Once the appropriate solutions have been identified, the current value stream map is amended to include the proposed changes. This new value stream map is referred to as the "future state value stream map."

Step three: Improve the process

Now that you have created a future state value stream map, you have to expose it to all the stakeholders and gain consensus on the proposed changes to the process. Once everyone is in agreement, the changes are implemented in order of priority. The employees must also be trained on how to handle the new process.

Step four: Sustain the changes

The final step is to make sure that the implemented changes are constantly monitored and verified. The appropriate key performance indicators should be used to establish and measure cost and performance-related parameters.

As you can see, there are many tools that are used when planning and implementing Six Sigma.

If you are using these tools for the DMAIC framework, make sure that you select the appropriate one. This will guarantee you credible results.

In the next chapter, you will learn how to implement Six Sigma in an organization.

Chapter Three: Implementing Six Sigma

No two organizations are exactly alike. They may exist within the same market or industry, but they face different sets of challenges. Therefore, the strategies that they use when implementing Six Sigma will vary significantly, especially if you consider their organizational culture and strategic goals.

In this chapter, you will learn how Six Sigma can be implemented within an organization and how to get top management to commit and support it. You will also learn how to reduce lead time to improve customer satisfaction and ensure business success.

There are generally two approaches that an organization can use when implementing Six Sigma:

- Execute a Six Sigma initiative or program

- Establish a Six Sigma infrastructure

Executing a Six Sigma Initiative or Program

This option involves training specific employees on how to apply Six Sigma tools in the workplace. It is an unstructured way of implementing Six Sigma in an organization.

A few practitioners are chosen and trained on how to use statistical tools whenever they feel that it is necessary to apply the tool. If the Six Sigma practitioners get stuck, they can ask a statistician for help.

Though this approach may yield some successes within the company, these are few and far between. The simple reason is that there is not enough consistency, and therefore, each success fails to provide the support for the next one. It is as if there is a lack of total commitment to fully implement the Six Sigma methodology throughout the organization.

An organization that focuses on implementing Six Sigma as a mere program will only change a few of their tools and introduce a couple of training classes for the affected employees. If it were to go further, it might apply these tools to a number of special projects. However, these projects are rarely a core part of the organization.

These projects tend to be low-level initiatives that have not even been endorsed by top management. If the solution that the project is meant to provide directly affects upper management, then it is possible that the project will experience a lot of internal resistance.

It is clear to see that implementing Six Sigma through tools alone is not likely to boost the bottom line or add value to the long-term, strategic goals of the organization.

This approach usually leads to Six Sigma being viewed as a fashionable methodology that is only useful during certain seasons. There will be a minimal return on the investment made to train employees.

No matter what kind of extraordinary achievements are made through the use of Six Sigma tools, the benefits will not be visible to top management. Their resistance to Six Sigma ultimately kills any attempts to bring change, and with no assigned change champion, even getting funds to finance the initiative becomes tough.

Ultimately, success can only be achieved by convincing upper management to support Six Sigma implementation throughout the organization.

Establishing a Six Sigma Infrastructure

The best way to implement Six Sigma in an organization is to focus on establishing a solid infrastructure that will guide all Six Sigma projects. This goes way beyond just introducing a couple of statistical tools that are used haphazardly. This particular option focuses on gaining top management buy-in before any investment in Six Sigma is made.

Employees are trained to use the right tools at the right time when working on a predefined project. Six Sigma practitioners are selected and trained for a period of four months, and in between training sessions, they are given projects to help them apply what they have learned.

An organization that invests time and money to deploy Six Sigma as part of its broader business strategy will benefit more than the one that simply deploys Six Sigma tools. Here are some of the benefits of deploying Six Sigma infrastructure with the support of upper management:

- The projects deployed directly affect the bottom line, thus achieving a bigger impact

- Six Sigma tools are used more effectively, efficiently, and productively

- It provides a project management strategy that practitioners can study and improve upon

- It makes it easier for the practitioners and upper management to communicate

- Critical business processes can be understood in detail

- It helps managers and employees understand the real value of statistical tools to the organization

One of the key steps in deploying a Six Sigma project is the project selection process. It is important to select projects that will help the organization meet its strategic business goals. Six Sigma can be a useful and effective roadmap for achieving these goals.

Regardless of how an organization chooses to implement Six Sigma, the important thing to note is that Six Sigma should be a long-term commitment. This will ensure that there is an objective analysis of every element in the business process.

It will be easier to learn from past mistakes and improve on subsequent implementation plans. This will create a closed feedback loop that ultimately reaps dividends for the organization.

Overcoming Upper Management Reluctance

There are certain measures that you can take to overcome top management resistance to Six Sigma. Here are five steps to take to gain management support:

1. Choose your projects wisely – If you develop the right project selection criteria, you stand a better chance of picking projects that will have the greatest impact on the company's bottom line. This will prove to top management that Six Sigma is of value.

2. Get quick results – Make sure that the project bears fast results and generates significant returns. You will have about five weeks to show management that you can reduce costs and improve productivity by at least 30 percent.

3. Track your interim progress – Develop a work plan that specifies key milestones, responsibilities, and deliverables.

4. Gather an expert team – You may have to seek Six Sigma experts from within or outside the organization as part of your deployment team. Having qualified professionals increases the chances of project success. This will convince top management to consider implementing Six Sigma throughout the entire organization.

5. Maintain a clearly defined project scope – Make sure that the project scope is wide enough to generate significant returns but also narrow enough to enable quick completion.

Once top management sees the practical benefits of Six Sigma, they may consider a limited initial commitment or a broad-based rollout of Six Sigma throughout the organization.

Lead Time

Lead time is defined as the time from which the customer places an order to the moment the product or service is delivered. Every type of business has some form of lead time, whether it is in manufacturing, project management, software development, supply chain management, etc. The only difference is how lead time is interpreted in that particular industry.

But why is lead time so important in business?

Because time is money!

Let's say that a manufacturer usually buys steel from a supplier. Imagine a situation where the supplier has a lead time of one month. This means that the supplier takes one month to deliver an order for steel to the manufacturer.

Therefore, the manufacturer needs to maintain an inventory of one month's worth of steel to keep producing products for their customers.

Maintaining inventory means paying storage costs for the steel, so the longer the supplier's lead time, the greater the storage charges. It would be in the manufacturer's best interest to find a supplier who can supply the steel within a shorter period of time.

A longer lead time is also disadvantageous because it forces the manufacturer to be more precise with their demand forecast. If customer demand exceeds the forecast, delivery of products to the customers will be delayed. This will cause customer dissatisfaction. This is why reducing lead time is very important in business.

Components of lead time

Lead time consists of several different elements that originate from the various departments within an organization. These include:

- Preprocessing time – This is the time it takes to receive an order from the customer, understand the order, and then create a purchase order.

- Waiting time – The time an item has to spend awaiting production

- Processing time – The time it takes to produce an item

- Inspection time – The time it takes to check a product for conformity to standards

- Storage time – The amount of time an item stays in the factory or warehouse

- Transportation time – The amount of time the product is in transit from the factory to the customer

When you add up all these elements, you end up with the total lead time. One assumption that is made is that there is no inventory in storage. In other words, we assume that the product must be made from scratch.

So the challenge you have is to find a way to reduce the lead time.

How to reduce lead time

1. Eliminate non-value activities – Use value stream mapping to find those activities that do not add value to the process and eliminate them.

2. Simplify the production process – When you make the process less complex, production flows faster.

3. Improve layout – Arrange the machinery and work process such that raw materials and finished goods do not have to move long distances.

4. Document your operating procedure – Create a document for standard operating procedures so that every employee is familiar with what is required. This will enable quick learning, less confusion, and enhanced consistency.

5. Planned machinery maintenance – It is better to schedule the regular maintenance of machinery than to wait for a total shutdown that will cripple production.

6. Find backup suppliers – Create an arrangement with a group of suppliers so that in case one supplier lets you down, you can rely on another. Take time to educate your suppliers on how your operations are run so that they understand how important they are in your business process.

The truth is that customers will always gravitate toward companies that have shorter lead times. Any organization that works to reduce its lead time will ultimately improve its chances of success.

In the next chapter, you will learn the steps necessary to apply the DMAIC framework.

Chapter Four: The DMAIC Process

By now it should be clear that a Six Sigma project is designed to measure and improve the current performance level of a business process by using statistical tools.

As we mentioned earlier in chapter 2, DMAIC is the framework that is often used when implementing Six Sigma in an organization. In this chapter, you are going to learn more about the phases of DMAIC and the steps that are involved in each phase of the process.

DMAIC is an acronym that stands for Define, Measure, Analyze, improve, and Control.

It is simply a management system that allows an organization to generate a continuous flow of improvements to projects. DMAIC helps to determine which projects should be implemented as solutions to eliminate defects and produce sustainable results.

Prior to deploying any Six Sigma project, every business process must be assessed to determine which one will have the greatest impact on costs, quality, and efficiency. DMAIC is then used to identify a project that will reduce costs while improving efficiency and quality.

Phases of DMAIC

Define

This is the first phase of the DMAIC approach. In the Define phase, the goal is to clarify every single element that will be involved in the project. Here are the steps involved in the Define phase:

1. Creating a project charter and scope – This is a document that establishes the boundaries of the project. Since you cannot solve all the problems in a business process, you must define the limits of the project activities before moving forward.

2. Developing a high-level process map – This map is usually created using the SIPOC (Suppliers, Inputs, Process, Outputs, Customers) format. Once the map is complete, the project team can choose one specific area and create a more detailed plan.

3. Defining the customers, their requirements, and their expectations (CTQs) – It is important to understand who your customer is and the needs that they have. You have to reach out to your customers and get relevant feedback on how to best solve the problem.

4. Developing the problem statement and goals – A problem statement is a clear description of the challenges that the project seeks to address. You need to collect data that proves the existence of a problem and whether it is of a high or low priority. The problem statement should also include customer requirements, goals, and benefits that will accrue at the end of the project.

5. Defining the resources to be used – Project resources that need to be identified include the project sponsor, change champion, the process team, and any other material/financial resources that will be required.

6. Developing the project plan and its milestones – This should include a short statement of how the project activities will be completed, by whom, and the relevant timelines. You also need to specify the communication channels to be used.

Measure

In the Measure phase, the project team reviews and measures the state of the existing process. They create a baseline that will be used to determine the level of improvement after the project. Here are the steps involved in the Measure phase:

1. Create a detailed process map – A process map that is detailed will help the project team easily identify the areas in the process that have bottlenecks, defects, or useless steps.

2. Creating a data collection plan – Before you start collecting data, you first need to define the methods you will use and the objectives of the process. What metrics will be measured? What are the measuring tools that will be used? How often will measurements be taken? How will the data be recorded?

3. Gathering data – The data to be collected must be useful in defining the problem. It must also help in identifying the root causes and location of the problem.

4. Verifying the measurement system – The system you will use to measure the current state of the process needs to be reliable. It, therefore, must be analyzed. If you fail to validate your measuring system, you will end up collecting misleading information.

Analyze

The goal of this phase is to spot all the factors that may be responsible for the defects, waste, and bottlenecks. This will help you identify the root cause of the problem.

This can be accomplished by analyzing the data collected during the previous phase or reviewing additional information. Here are the steps involved in the Analyze phase:

1. Identifying value-added and non-value added process steps – The project team has to look closely at every step in the business process. The goal here is to identify which steps add value and which ones do not. Non-value added steps must then be targeted for elimination.

2. Identifying sources of variation – Sources of variation are simply the causal factors that may be responsible for a defect, bottleneck, or waste. This can be achieved through brainstorming and other tools. Once you have compiled a list of causal factors, you should rank them and then investigate the major ones.

3. Determining the root cause – One of the challenges of problem-solving is that there are times when the perceived problem keeps recurring. If this happens in Six Sigma, it is because the project team solved a symptom and not the root cause of the problem. You have to identify the root cause out of all the potential causal factors. Then you have to develop effective countermeasures using the tools available.

At the end of the Analyze phase, any new information found should be used to update the project charter.

Improve

This is the phase in which a solution is identified and developed. This is only possible after all the relevant data has been collected and analyzed.

The goal is to come up with a list of possible ideas and then select the most suitable one. Here are the steps involved in this phase:

1. Performing experiments - The project team investigates how the possible root causes can be resolved to improve the process.

2. Creating innovative solutions – The project team identifies potential solutions that will improve quality, boost safety, lower costs, and enhance efficiency. Of course, the best solutions should be able to achieve all this without consuming too many resources.

3. Assessing failure modes of potential solutions – Each potential solution should be reviewed in terms of risk and possible impact. This will help the team to identify any problems that may occur when a solution is implemented. The best solution should be low-risk and have no negative impact on the process.

4. Selecting the preferred solution – The best solution is picked and then implemented.

5. Re-evaluating potential solution – The solution that has been selected is validated to confirm whether it has improved the process and resolved all issues. This is done using statistical methods, data collection, or pilot builds.

Control

The Control phase is all about maintaining the solution. The strategy is to constantly monitor the performance of the new process and how employees are responding to it.

This should never be a one-off event. All the data collected by the process management team should be compiled and used to create a manual that will be used to improve subsequent projects and teach new staff members.

Here are the steps involved in this phase:

1. Updating the process standards – Once improvements have been made to the process, it is important to document all the changes and create new standards. These updates can be in the form of control plans, work instructions, etc.

2. Implementing statistical process control – This is a way to track how the primary steps in the process are performing. The process owner or associates should be able to note any shifts in the process.

3. Verifying benefits, cost savings, and growth of profits – A process monitoring plan should be created to track and record the *long-term* performance of the new process. This plan must clarify how the new process will be measured, the frequency of measurement, the person responsible for fixing any issues, a method of documentation, etc.

4. Celebrating – Once the project is over, it is important that the whole team comes together to celebrate. Upper management should also recognize the efforts made and benefits realized.

At the end of the Control phase, the new process should be handed over to the process owner. If there are any opportunities to improve other processes, this would be a good time to discuss such issues.

The DMAIC framework is an effective way to implement Six Sigma.

The important thing to remember is not to try to resolve every problem at once. Stick to the project scope and follow the right steps carefully.

In the next chapter, you will learn how to identify and launch a project.

Chapter Five: Identifying and Launching a Project

In this chapter, you will learn how to identify and select a project that will successfully improve a process. You will also learn some of the factors that need to be considered before launching a project.

While many organizations understand how to choose process improvement projects, they fail to utilize the right methods when identifying projects.

Preconditions for Identifying a Project

Before they identify a project, the project team has to evaluate the ideas available. There are four key steps that must be followed before identifying a project:

1. Acknowledge the strategic plan of the organization – The project team must understand the long-term strategic interests of the organization so that they identify a project that matches those same goals. This is an intensive process that includes assessing the interests of stakeholders, gauging the organization's financial capacity, developing contingency plans in case of market fluctuations, and drafting an action plan.

2. Align the project goals with the strategic plan of the business – The project itself will have specific tasks and activities, which must align with the specific action plans of the organization.

3. Integrate the organization's strategic plan into the deployment system – When a Six Sigma project is being deployed, the high-level goals must be broken down to create functional goals.

These functional goals are then deployed to individual departments throughout the organization.

4. Identify the core processes of the business - Every business has core processes that involve converting an input into an output that customers are willing to pay for. The project team must recognize these core processes and break them down until the actual work steps can be seen. It is these lower-level work steps that are then targeted for improvement. The improvement project must be able to boost the performance of the work steps.

How to Identify a Project

The process of identifying and selecting a Six Sigma project should be a collaborative effort between the Project Champion and the Master Black Belt.

In the previous section, we talked about the preconditions that must be satisfied before project identification. Once the core processes and work steps have been understood, the next steps should be:

1. The Champion and Master Black Belt sit down and brainstorm to come up with ideas. At this stage, every potential improvement opportunity should be put on the table.

2. Once a list of improvement ideas has been generated, they should be ranked and prioritized according to their alignment with strategic goals, their risk, and their potential returns.

3. The list of ideas with their rankings is presented to the project team. This is done to build consensus.

4. The best project idea is selected and the team prepares itself for project launch.

Launching a Six Sigma Project

When a Six Sigma project is being launched, the main objective is to ensure that there will be tangible results according to the implementation schedule and available resources. In the early stages of launch, the project sponsor plays a major role because they tend to be involved in the majority of the decisions made.

The project Champion is also actively engaged with the deployment leader and project team. The relevant people have to work hard to make sure that adequate resources are made available.

With that said, there are three major factors that impact the launch of every project. These are:

- How well defined the project is – It is important to define exactly what the project is supposed to address. It is also necessary to specify the sector or function of the organization that the project directly affects.

- The clarity of the project's scope – It is important to be clear on the limits of the project because this will impact the project schedule. If a project has a well-defined scope, it is usually completed on time. Therefore, make sure that the scope is limited to problems that are related to a particular process.

- The resources available to the project – Resources can be manpower, money, equipment, and the like. For example, when talking about manpower, there has to be a distinction between the core team and the support staff. The core team should consist of 4 to 7 individuals who directly influence or are impacted by the process. This can even include a supplier who supplies raw materials for the process being improved.

However, the support staff can include about 10 to 20 other individuals who assist the core team.

Identifying and launching a Six Sigma project needs to be done in an orderly manner to ensure project success.

The right ideas must be developed, the right projects selected, and the right individuals involved. Project definition, scope, and resources must also be considered during launch.

Any organization that considers these factors should be able to implement an improvement project successfully.

In the next chapter, you will learn how to understand the customer.

Chapter Six: Understanding Your Customer

One of the fundamental tenets of business is that you must always satisfy the needs of the customer. The top management of an organization will tell you that they are already doing this.

But how true is this statement? For you to meet the needs of your customer, you must first know who they are, and the truth is that there are some organizations that don't even recognize who their customers are.

Many opponents of Six Sigma talk about how it slows down the organization's ability to meet customer needs.

But in this chapter, you will learn how Six Sigma plays a significant role in identifying customers and their needs. Six Sigma can actually help you hear and understand the voice of your customer.

The Real Customers

If you want to know who your real customers are, you have to consider three questions:

- Who is the primary customer? – This one should be simple enough to answer correctly, but sadly, many companies get it wrong. They think that just because they are selling their products or services to a distributor, then the distributor is their primary customer. The truth is that the end-user is their primary customer. If the end-user feels that a product is not able to satisfy their needs, they will shift allegiance to a different brand. In this case, both the distributor and the company will suffer.

- Do different customers have similar pain points? - There are some customers that will have similar needs, and others may have different pain points. An organization must discern which needs are similar and which ones are different. The next step after this should be to determine how each of these needs affect profits and re-prioritize accordingly.

- Which customers are worth more? – There are times when a company must measure the value of each of their customers. This will help in determining which customer needs to cater for first and which ones to push to the back burner for a while. It is always a good idea to take a long-term perspective when deciding which needs come first. Therefore, the customers that will bring in greater revenue in the long-term are worth more.

Once you know which factors to consider, you can then group your customers: There are two broad categories of customers:

1. Internal customers – Internal customers can be found within the organization, for example, employees, management, or even entire departments.

2. External customers – External customers include the end-consumers of a product or service, the shareholders, and other clients. These are people who either use the products or services directly or have a vested interest in the activities of the organization. They are usually found outside the organization.

Voice of the Customer

This is simply a reference to the comments, preferences, and expectations of your customers. Voice of the customer, or VOC, is actually a process that an organization uses to collect information from customers. The goal is to understand what customers think about a product or service and then make the necessary improvements in quality.

VOC comes in two forms – spoken and unspoken. Customers can express their preferences verbally but sometimes, they can express their comments through body language and behavior. This means that the methods used to collect feedback from customers must be capable of capturing both forms of VOC.

When the VOC is captured, the information must then be converted into customer needs and customer requirements. Needs and requirements are not the same.

A customer's needs are their desires about a particular product or service. A requirement refers to the attribute of a product or service that satisfies a need.

For example, a customer may require an air conditioner to keep their room cool during hot weather. In this case, their need is cool temperature inside the room.

At the same time, the customer may want the air conditioner to be affordable and easy to maintain. It is important for the project team to focus on the need and consider the wants to be non-essential.

The reason for this is simple. If the project team provides a product or service that meets the customer's needs but doesn't satisfy their wants, the customer may be unhappy, but they will still buy the product or service.

However, if their wants are met but their need is not fulfilled, the customer will choose to go to a rival company to get their needs met.

On the other hand, a requirement is a "must have" feature of a product or service. The air conditioner must have features that enable it to keep a room cool. Therefore, the customer needs are used to create products or services that satisfy specific requirements.

Classes of VOC

There are four distinct classes of VOC. These are:

- Voice of Associate – This is the feedback obtained from employees within the organization

- Voice of Investor – The project team can also receive feedback from shareholders and management of an organization

- Voice of Customer – This is the feedback that the project team receives from clients and end-users

- Voice of Process – This kind of feedback comes from the process that needs to be improved

The four categories above are usually referred to by the acronym AICP (Associate, Investor, Customer, and Process). In order to collect the voices of AICP, the project team will have to rely on certain methods of gathering data.

Methods of Collecting VOC

1. Surveys – These are questionnaires that the project team will send out to existing and potential customers. Surveys tend to be cheap, but the problem is that they have a low response rate. Most respondents rarely return the questionnaires back to the team.

2. Interviews – These are face-to-face meetings with existing and potential customers. The customers are asked a series of questions and feedback is gathered. Interviews are useful for tackling complex issues. However, the interviewer must be well trained.

3. Focus groups – A focus group is a group of people who are gathered in one room and a specific topic is discussed. Everyone contributes their opinion about a product or service. Focus groups are great for identifying the requirements that are critical to the quality of a product/service. However, it is difficult to generalize the feedback received.

4. Suggestions – The customers can be questioned and asked to provide their suggestions about a product or service. The project team evaluates the suggestions but is not required to consider them when selecting a solution. The suggestions are simply viewed as improvement opportunities.

5. Observations – Instead of the project team asking customers questions to gain feedback, they simply watch how employees and clients interact with a process or product. The observed information is then used as a VOC.

The main goal of Voice of the Customer is to obtain the needs of all the customers. But first, you have to know who your customers are before you start analyzing their needs. Do not assume that you can rely on past history or experience.

The way organizations interact with customers has changed. A long time ago, everything was about the organization and customer needs came last.

Today, the customer is king and most business relations are customer-centric. In the future, the customer and the organization will be enjoined. Organizational and customer needs will be merged into one.

In the next chapter, you will learn about the do's and don'ts of Six Sigma.

Chapter Seven: 10 Six Sigma Do's and Don'ts

Any organization that wants to implement Six Sigma must be willing to follow a systematic approach. There are many organizations that merely use Six Sigma as a way to market and promote their products but are not really interested in applying it as a long-term business initiative.

Such organizations have failed to realize the value and benefits of Six Sigma.

In this chapter, you will learn about some of the things that an organization should do and some of the mistakes that must be avoided. All throughout this book, you have slowly learned what to do and how to adopt a Six Sigma approach.

But you also need to keep an eye on the assumptions and useless approaches that some organizations make. These pitfalls tend to be disastrous for the organization, and a failed Six Sigma initiative can have terrible financial repercussions.

With that said, let's look at 10 do's and don'ts when deploying Six Sigma.

The 10 Do's of Six Sigma

1. Do explain why you need to adopt a Six Sigma approach – The first thing you must do is establish a clear reason why Six Sigma is needed and how it will benefit the entire organization. This will help you convince not just the upper management but the lower level employees as well.

2. Do get the support and engagement of upper management –
    Make sure that top management is sold on the idea of
    improving the current processes. Once the organization's
    executive team understands the potential of Six Sigma, they will
    provide the impetus needed to make it a success.

3. Do ensure proper project planning – You have to think things
    through before taking any action. This is one of the benefits of
    using the DMAIC framework. It forces you to define, measure,
    and analyze the problem and come up with the best solution
    possible.

4. Do create a robust project selection system – The project team
    must start things off on the right foot. This means they have to
    ensure that the right project is selected based on reliable data
    and strategic business goals.

5. Do choose the best candidates for Six Sigma training – You
    cannot train the whole organization when deploying Six Sigma.
    Therefore, pick employees who have a keen interest in Six
    Sigma and train them so that they can transfer that knowledge
    to other employees. With time, the majority of employees will
    have gained practical knowledge of the Six Sigma methodology.

6. Do select a capable Champion – Every Six Sigma initiative
    must be led by a Six Sigma Champion. This should be someone
    who is trained in Six Sigma and is passionate about its
    implementation within the organization. It will be the
    Champion's responsibility to get everyone else excited about
    the changes and benefits that Six Sigma will bring.

7. Do involve all relevant stakeholders – Implementing Six Sigma
    needs to be a collaborative effort if it is to succeed. Everyone,
    including the lowest level employees, customers, and suppliers
    should be involved in the implementation process. The process

owner or sponsor should also be consulted in every phase of DMAIC.

8. Do ensure maximum communication – There must be effective communication at all levels of the organization. This will ensure that everyone stays in the loop and no department feels isolated or left out during implementation.

9. Do review the deployment regularly – Once the improvement project has been implemented, it must be monitored regularly to ensure that everything stays on track. This will enable any deviations to be identified early and corrected.

10. Do celebrate your success – After you successfully implement that first Six Sigma project, make sure that you celebrate the victory. Success tends to be contagious, so when people recognize and praise the victory, greater interest in the Six Sigma approach will be developed.

The 10 Don'ts of Six Sigma

1. Don't let Six Sigma be a fad – Some organizations view Six Sigma as a way to appear in tune with current best practices, so they use a few tools for a while but don't fully adopt the methodology. Any organization that does this will never realize the full potential of Six Sigma.

2. Don't assume that you are different – Many organizations refuse to adopt Six Sigma because they believe that they won't get the same results as other organizations. While it is true that every organization is unique, Six Sigma can still work and benefit any business.

3. Don't hire part-time Black Belts – One common assumption is that Six Sigma Black Belts can work as part-timers and the project will still proceed at a good pace. This is a mistake because, without a full-time Black Belt, the project will not generate the momentum required to bring change to the organization.

4. Don't implement without a deployment leader – The role of the deployment leader is to train the project team, assign tasks, and choose the Six Sigma tools. If there is no deployment leader, there will be confusion and conflict that will ultimately result in failure. The team members will begin to focus on their own areas and there will be a lack of genuine synergy.

5. Don't get greedy – One of the main reasons why a Six Sigma project ends in failure is scope creep. If you get greedy and try to fix every problem in the organization, you will fail. Avoid making the project scope too broad. Otherwise, the project team will easily be overwhelmed.

6. Don't focus on isolated implementation – Six Sigma is best used as a tool for improving an entire process rather than just a single product or service. Isolated implementation may be a worthwhile idea if an organization lacks adequate resources, but it is not a smart strategy in the long run. You cannot actualize the full benefits of Six Sigma through small and disconnected improvement projects.

7. Don't obsess over Six Sigma training – The common assumption is that everyone involved in executing a project must be trained and certified in every tool and technique. This is not true. There are a lot of Six Sigma courses and complex tools that are being taught, but you don't need all of them to make your project a success. It is better to focus on learning

and applying what is relevant to your project. There shouldn't be an obsession with the number of Belts in the project team.

8. Don't ignore technology – Technology plays a critical role in implementing a Six Sigma project. Technology makes it easier to measure, analyze and control systems and processes that need to be or have already been improved. It would be unwise to try to separate the two.

9. Don't forget to validate the measurement systems – Six Sigma is built on the foundation of hard data and precise measurements. However, don't fall into the trap of blindly following a measurement system without verifying it.

10. Exaggerating the opportunity counts – Sometimes Six Sigma practitioners try to exaggerate the number of opportunities there are in a process. This is usually an attempt to fabricate their performance so that stakeholders will believe that the process has improved significantly. This kind of deception is wrong.

Conclusion

Now that you have come to the end of the book, I hope that you appreciate everything that Six Sigma stands for. Over the years, there have been a lot of myths and confusion regarding this particular methodology.

However, one thing should be clear by now. Six Sigma is extremely useful for any organization that wants to improve quality, reduce costs, and enhance the speed of delivery of goods and services.

You have learned the most important tools and processes that are used in Six Sigma implementation. Keep them in mind as you move on to the next phase of the journey – which should be implementing and deploying a Six Sigma project.

Remember to follow the right procedure when trying to identify a solution to defects in your business process. Use the DMAIC stages to guide you every step of the way.

If there is any information that is not clear, feel free to go through the chapter again. Make sure you understand what needs to be done before you start any Six Sigma initiative.

I hope that you will take action to use Six Sigma to achieve the strategic goals of your organization.

Good luck!

Resources

http://asq.org/learn-about-quality/six-sigma/implementing.html

https://quality-one.com/six-sigma/

www.graphicproducts.com/articles/six-sigma-principles/

https://www.business2community.com/strategy/5-benefits-six-sigma-01765393

https://sixsigmastudyguide.com/value-stream-mapping/

http://asq.org/learn-about-quality/six-sigma/implementing.html

http://www.whatissixsigma.net/lead-time/

http://www.isme.in/ten-essential-dos-and-do-nots-of-six-sigma/

https://goleansixsigma.com/3-important-factors-to-consider-when-launching-a-successful-lean-six-sigma-project/

http://www.six-sigma-material.com/Voice-of-the-Customer.html

https://sixsigmastudyguide.com/voice-of-customer-voice-of-client-voc/